OXFORD SPELLING

Dr Tessa Daffern

STUDENT
BOOK
4

Name: _____

Class: _____

OXFORD
UNIVERSITY PRESS
AUSTRALIA & NEW ZEALAND

OXFORD
UNIVERSITY PRESS

Oxford University Press is a department of the University of Oxford.
It furthers the University's objective of excellence in research,
scholarship, and education by publishing worldwide. Oxford is a registered
trademark of Oxford University Press in the UK and in certain other
countries.

Published in Australia by
Oxford University Press
Level 8, 737 Bourke Street, Docklands, Victoria 3008, Australia.

© Oxford University Press 2021

The moral rights of the author have been asserted

First published 2021

Reprinted 2024

ISBN 9780190326128

Reproduction and communication for educational purposes
The Australian *Copyright Act 1968* (the Act) allows educational institutions that
are covered by remuneration arrangements with Copyright Agency to reproduce
and communicate certain material for educational purposes. For more information,
see copyright.com.au.

Edited by Laura Rentsch
Cover illustration by Lisa Hunt
Illustrated by Becky Davies
Typeset by Integra Software Services Pvt. Ltd., Pondicherry, India
Proofread by Anita Mullick
Printed in China by Leo Paper Products Ltd

MIX
Paper | Supporting
responsible forestry
FSC® C020056
FSC
www.fsc.org

Acknowledgements
Things That Are Most in the World by Judi Barrett, illustrated by John Nickle, Simon & Schuster, 2001; *The Shaggy
Gully Times* by Jackie French, illustrated by Bruce Whatley, Harper Collins Australia, 2010; *Pencil of Doom* by Andy
Griffiths, illustrated by Terry Denton, Pan Macmillan Australia, 2013; *Ziba Came on a Boat* by Liz Lofthouse,
illustrated by Robert Ingpen, Picture Puffin, Penguin Books Australia, 2012; *Withering-by-Sea* by Judith Rossell,
Harper Collins Publishers Australia, 2014; Shutterstock for photographs on pp. 26, 35, 82, 88.

The 'Bringing it together' activities provided online are adapted with permission from Daffern, T. (2018).
The components of spelling: Instruction and assessment for the linguistic inquirer. Literacy Education Solutions Pty Limited.

Every effort has been made to trace the original source of copyright material contained in this book. The
publisher will be pleased to hear from copyright holders to rectify any errors or omissions.

WELCOME TO OXFORD SPELLING

Welcome to *Oxford Spelling Student Book* 4! This book contains 28 units that you will use across the year, and that will help you gain new spelling knowledge and skills.

You will notice that each unit is divided into three sections:

- **Phonology (green section)**
- **Orthography (blue section)**
- **Morphology (purple section).**

This has been done to guide you in the types of thinking you might use to answer the questions in each section.

- In the phonology sections, think about the sounds you can hear in words.
- In the orthography sections, think about the letter patterns that you know.
- In the morphology sections, think about the meaning of base words, prefixes and suffixes.

At the end of each unit, your teacher will work with you on a 'Bringing it together' activity. This is a chance to bring together all the things you are learning about spelling and apply them to new words!

Your teacher, along with the *Oxford Spelling* superheroes, will be giving you lots of helpful information as you work through this book. Look out for the tips in each unit for handy hints on how to answer questions.

Enjoy *Oxford Spelling*, and meet the two superheroes who will help you become super spellers – Gooey Gigi and Magnetic Max!

UNIT 1

Phonology

Tip A phoneme is the smallest speech sound you can hear. For example, the word 'shop' has three phonemes: **/sh/**, **/o/**, **/p/**.

1 Count the syllables in each word. Sort the words using the table and then count the phonemes in each word.

| peasant | prince | brick | China | tiny | remote |

| village | bleak | house | homemade | kite | lived |

Tip All syllables have a vowel phoneme.

One-syllable words	Number of phonemes	Two-syllable words	Number of phonemes

OXFORD UNIVERSITY PRESS

Tip

Remember to check the glossary if you come across a spelling term you don't know.

2 What is a schwa?

_____

_____

3 Each of these words has a schwa. Underline the letters in each word that represent a schwa.

| peasant | London | starvation |

1 Look in a book you are reading in class. Find words with the **/m/** phoneme and look at the different letter patterns that can spell this sound. Write some of the words in the table.

m as in 'make'	
mb as in 'thumb'	
mm as in 'command'	
mn as in 'column'	

2 Look again at the letter patterns that represent the **/m/** phoneme in the words you wrote in the last activity.

    a What is the most common letter pattern? _____

    b What is the least common letter pattern? _____

    c What can you notice about the position of each letter pattern in the words you wrote? Are some letter patterns more common at the beginning or end of words? For example, are you likely to see **mm** at the start of a word?

_____

_____

_____

_____

Morphology

1 What is a homophone?

_____

_____

2 Write a definition for each homophone.

practice	
practise	

Tip

Use a dictionary to check you are using the correct homophone.

Dictionary

4

A verb is a word for something that happens. 'Play' is a verb in the sentence 'I play hockey'.

Tip

If you are unsure whether to use 'practise' or 'practice', try using the verbs *to prepare* (or *preparing, prepared, prepares*), *to rehearse* (or *rehearsing, rehearsed, rehearses*) or *to repeat* (or *repeating, repeated, repeats*) instead. If the sentence still makes sense, then 'practise' is most probably correct. If it doesn't, then use 'practice'.

3 Complete the sentences using the correct homophone.

| practice | practise |

a The flute player likes to _____ with the band.

b You can improve your writing with lots of _____.

c A doctor with a private _____ will

_____ privately.

4 Write a sentence using each homophone.

practise	
practice	

Now try this unit's 'Bringing it together' activity, which your teacher will give you.

UNIT 2

1 Count the syllables in each word. Sort the words using the table and then count the phonemes in each word.

whispers   gentle   reflected   riverbank   answer

stringybarks   rejoices   melting   company

magpie   shadow   loneliness

Two-syllable words	Number of phonemes	Three-syllable words	Number of phonemes

OXFORD UNIVERSITY PRESS

> **Tip**
>
> A digraph is two letters that represent one speech sound. **Th** is a digraph in the word 'that'.
>
> A schwa is a common vowel sound that is not long or short. Instead it is an **/uh/** sound. It can be heard in some unaccented syllables. For example, the **a** in 'balloon' represents a schwa.

2 Read the words below. Underline the consonant digraphs. Circle two words that have a syllable with a schwa.

whispers	gentle	reflected	riverbank	answer	stringybarks
rejoices	melting	company	magpie	shadow	loneliness

1 Look in a book you are reading in class. Find words with the **/n/** phoneme and look at the different letter patterns that can spell this sound. Write some of the words in the table.

n as in 'nice'	
gn as in 'gnome'	
kn as in 'knot'	
nn as in 'annoy'	

2 Look again at the letter patterns that represent the **/n/** phoneme in the words you wrote in the last activity.

a What is the most common letter pattern? _____

b What is the least common letter pattern? _____

c What can you notice about the position of each letter pattern in the words you wrote? Are some letter patterns more common at the beginning or end of words? For example, can a word end with the digraph **gn**?

_____

_____

_____

_____

3 Find the words in the word search.

t	n	g	u	u	r	h	a	y	d
v	s	i	g	n	s	v	n	b	o
z	c	a	f	f	e	i	n	e	n
n	i	c	e	t	q	j	o	w	e
h	b	a	n	n	e	r	y	h	k
a	c	a	m	p	a	i	g	n	n
l	v	d	i	n	n	e	r	p	o
i	y	d	e	s	n	k	p	f	t
g	g	o	n	e	g	n	o	m	e
n	d	c	o	n	n	e	c	t	l

caffeine   campaign

sign   banner

nice   knot

done   connect

align   gnome

gone   dinner

annoy

Tip

Homophones are words that sound the same but have a different spelling and meaning.

OXFORD UNIVERSITY PRESS

1 Write a definition for each homophone. You may use a dictionary to help you.

principle	
principal	

It can be tricky to remember the correct spelling of homophones. A mnemonic is a way to help you remember the spelling of tricky words. It could be a funny phrase, an acronym or a rhyme.

Tip

The following mnemonic may help you remember the spelling of the word 'principal', as in 'school principal':

Notice that the ending of the word is **pal**, and not **ple**. Think of a 'principal' as a 'pal'.

2 Complete the sentences using the correct homophone.

principle   principal

a The school _____ spoke to the students during the assembly.

b A person of _____ is truthful.

3 Write a sentence using each homophone.

principle	
principal	

Now try this unit's
'Bringing it together'
activity, which your teacher
will give you.

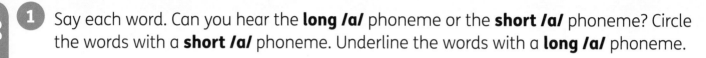

Phonology

1 Say each word. Can you hear the **long /a/** phoneme or the **short /a/** phoneme? Circle the words with a **short /a/** phoneme. Underline the words with a **long /a/** phoneme.

| persuades | magpie | riverbank | wakes | waiting | relax |

| races | shadow | clamped | blackness | rage |

2 Look in a book you are reading in class. Find five words with a **short /a/** phoneme, and five words with a **long /a/** phoneme. Write the words in the table.

Short /a/ phoneme	Long /a/ phoneme

Orthography

1 Choose two words from the list that you don't write very often. Write a definition for each one on the next page. You may use a dictionary to help you.

| tray | wait | rage | nation | persuade | vertebrae |

| mosaic | delay | weight | prey | conversation | quaint |

| great | clay | survey | plains | trade | stray |

| steak | favour | freight | they | parade | label |

Word	Definition

2 There are many ways to spell the **long /a/** phoneme. Find the letter patterns that spell the **long /a/** phoneme in the words from the last activity. Sort the words using the table.

Letter pattern	Word
ay	
ai	
a-e	
eigh	
a	
ae	
ey	
ea	

A base word is the smallest part of a word that is also a word on its own. 'Jump' is a base word. A suffix is a letter or letters that go at the end of a base word to make a new word: **-ing** is a suffix.

Tense tells us when something happened. Present tense means something is happening now. In the sentence 'I am jumping', 'jumping' is a present tense word. It describes an action happening now.

Tip

1 Use the rules to complete the activities about the suffixes **-s** and **-es**. Use the words to make present tense sentences. Then write your own sentences in present tense.

If the base word ends with a consonant graph, blend or digraph, but not s, x, z, ch or sh, add the suffix -s.   kick | kicks

kick	The toddler _____ the ball.
shout	

Tip

A trigraph is three letters that represent one speech sound. **tch** in the word 'itch' is a trigraph.

If the base word ends with s, x, z, ch, sh or a consonant trigraph such as tch, add the suffix -es.   mix | mixes

mix	The food processor _____ the ingredients together.
match	

If the base word ends in a consonant and then y, change the y to i and add the suffix -es.   fly | flies

fly	The paper aeroplane _____ to the other room.
marry	

If the base word **ends in** e, **just add the** suffix -s.   **hobble | hobbles**

hobble	A soccer player _____ off the field.
race	

Tip

Etymology is the study of where words come from and how they have changed over time.

2 Use an online etymology dictionary to research the origin of the words in the table. Write a definition for each word.

Word	Origin (place and time)	Definition
matinée		
purée		
entrée		

Now try this unit's 'Bringing it together' activity, which your teacher will give you.

UNIT 4

Phonology

1 Say each word. Can you hear the **short /e/** phoneme or the **long /e/** phoneme? Circle the words with a **short /e/** phoneme. Underline the words with a **long /e/** phoneme.

cent   beacon   kettle   regional   generational

seasonal   expression   eastern   western

entered   electrical   equal   increase   receive

2 Look in a book you are reading in class. Find some words with a **short /e/** phoneme and some words with a **long /e/** phoneme. Write the words in the table.

Short /e/ phoneme	Long /e/ phoneme

Orthography

1 Choose two words from the list that you don't write very often. Write a definition for each on the next page. You may use a dictionary to help you.

screen   team   genius   athlete   thief   receive

steep   seasonal   regional   delete   protein   theme

eagle   ceiling   eastern   achieve   speed   even

briefly   beef   feline   seize   concrete

Word	Definition

2 There are many ways to spell the **long /e/** phoneme. Find the letter patterns that spell the **long /e/** phoneme in the words from the last activity. Sort the words using the table.

ee	
ea	
ei	
e	
ie	
e-e	

1 Use the rules to complete the activities about the suffix **-ing**. Use the words to make **present** tense sentences. Then write your own sentences in **present** tense.

If the base word **ends with a short vowel** graph **then a consonant** graph, **double the last letter and add the** suffix **-ing.   clap | clapping**

clap	The audience is _____.
skid	

If the base word ends with x, or with a consonant blend, digraph or trigraph, just add the suffix -ing.   fix | fixing

| fix | The plumber is _____ our sink. |
| snatch | |

If the base word has a medial vowel digraph, just add -ing.   sleep | sleeping

| sleep | The bears are _____ in a cave. |
| droop | |

If the base word ends in y, or a vowel digraph or trigraph such as ow or igh, just add the suffix -ing.   fly | flying

| fly | I am _____ my new kite at the park. |
| sigh | |

If the base word ends in e, usually drop the e and then add the suffix -ing.   giggle | giggling

| giggle | They couldn't stop _____ at the silly rhyme. |
| smile | |

Now try this unit's 'Bringing it together' activity, which your teacher will give you.

UNIT 5

1 Say each word. Can you hear the **short /o/** phoneme or the **long /o/** phoneme? Circle the words with a **short /o/** phoneme. Underline the words with a **long /o/** phoneme.

doctor	ocean	prospect	snowing	complex

dispose	oxygen	contrast	approach	horizontal

explode	possibility	arrow	notice

2 Look in a book you are reading in class. Find some words with a **short /o/** phoneme and some words with a **long /o/** phoneme. Write the words in the table.

Short /o/ phoneme	Long /o/ phoneme

1 There are many ways to spell the **long /o/** phoneme. Find the letter patterns that spell the **long /o/** phoneme in the words. Sort the words using the table.

groan	bellow	compose	bonus	local	woe	dough
plateau	moan	corrode	hollow	though	roe	mellow
roam	cyclone	noble	bureau	gloat	although	
toe	gateau	bestow	notice	enclose	aloe	

oa	
ow	
o-e	
o	
oe	
ough	
eau	

OXFORD UNIVERSITY PRESS

2 Write these words in alphabetical order in the left column. Then write a definition for each word in the right column. You may use a dictionary to help you.

mellow	gloat	bellow	roe	bestow	roam

Word	Definition

1 Use an online etymology dictionary to research the origin of the words in the table. Write a definition for each word.

Word	Origin (place and time)	Definition
bureau		
plateau		
gateau		

2 Change each of the base words below by using suffixes. One is done for you.

When adding suffixes to the base words, remember to use the rules that you have learned so far.

Tip

Base word	+ Suffix **-s** or **-es**	+ Suffix **-ing**
dispose	disposes	disposing
approach		
explode		
bellow		
roam		
plateau		

3 Choose one of the base words from the last activity. Write a sentence using the word when it ends in the suffix **-s** or **-es**. Then write a sentence using the word when it ends in the suffix **-ing**.

a _____

_____

b _____

_____

Now try this unit's 'Bringing it together' activity, which your teacher will give you.

OXFORD UNIVERSITY PRESS

UNIT 6

1 Say each word. Can you hear the **short /oo/** phoneme or the **long /oo/** phoneme? Sort the words using the table.

| cocoon | booklet | cooking | acoustics |

| monsoon | footage | approve | soot |

| cruise | should | brutal | coupon |

| woodland | through | woollen | hook |

Short /oo/ phoneme as in 'shook'	**Long /oo/** phoneme as in 'boot'

2 Look in a book you are reading. Find some more words to add to the table above.

OXFORD UNIVERSITY PRESS

1 There are many ways to spell the **long /oo/** phoneme (as in the word 'boot'). Find the letter patterns that spell the **long /oo/** phoneme in the words. Sort the words using the table.

true   cocoon   prune   jewel   acoustics   truth   bruise

tomb   through   monsoon   approve   cruise   construe

coupon   sewage   crude   brutal

ue	
oo	
u-e	
ew	
ou	
u	
ui	
o	
ough	

2 Choose three words with different letter patterns from the last activity. Write a sentence for each word. Underline the word with the **long /oo/** phoneme in each sentence.

a _____

b _____

c _____

Verbs are words that tell us that something happens, such as an action.

Regular verbs are verbs that can have a suffix added to change tense.

Regular verbs in past tense are spelled using the suffix **-ed**. Sometimes the base verb needs to change when the suffix is added.

1 Use the rules to complete the activities about the suffix **-ed**. Use the words to make past tense sentences. Then write your own sentences in past tense.

> **If the base word ends with a short vowel graph then a consonant graph other than x, double the last letter and then add the suffix -ed.   flop | flopped**

flop	Hannah _____ onto the chair.
clap	

> **If the base word ends with x, or with a consonant blend, digraph or trigraph, just add the suffix -ed.   smash | smashed**

smash	The dinner plate _____ when it fell to the ground.
wash	

> **If the base word has a medial vowel digraph, just add the suffix -ed.   rain | rained**

rain	I stood under the umbrella while it _____.
gloat	

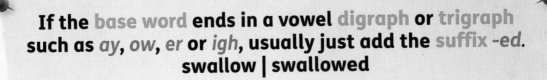

If the **base word** ends in a vowel **digraph** or **trigraph** such as *ay*, *ow*, *er* or *igh*, usually just add the **suffix** *-ed*.
swallow | swallowed

swallow	Antonio quickly _____ the tasty food.
bellow	

If the **base word** ends in *e*, drop the *e* and then add the **suffix** *-ed*.   wrinkle | wrinkled

wrinkle	My skin _____ after a long soak in the bath.
notice	

If the **base word** ends in a consonant and then *y*, change the *y* to *i* and add the **suffix** *-ed*.   copy | copied

copy	Ziba _____ the list of phone numbers.
worry	

Now try this unit's 'Bringing it together' activity, which your teacher will give you.

OS

OXFORD UNIVERSITY PRESS

UNIT 7

1 Say each word. Can you hear the **short /i/** phoneme or the **long /i/** phoneme? Sort the words using the table.

| demographic | satellite | cycle | reconciliation | environment |

| science | characteristics | multicultural | height | invasive |

| guide | ecological | predict | ripe | similar | twice |

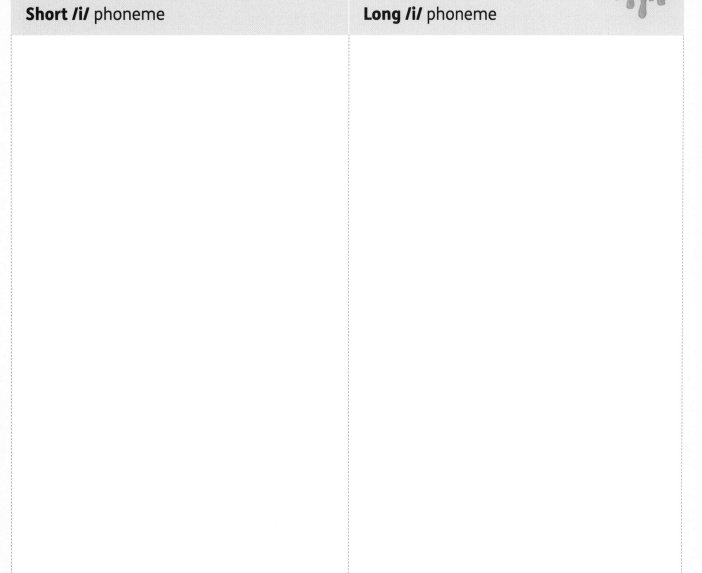

Short /i/ phoneme	**Long /i/** phoneme

2 Look in a book you are reading. Add some more words to the table above.

3 Count the syllables in each word from the last activity. Choose one word to write in each box.

One-syllable word	Two-syllable word	Three-syllable word

Four-syllable word	Five-syllable word	Six-syllable word

Orthography

1 There are many ways to spell the **long /i/** phoneme. Find the letter patterns that spell the **long /i/** phoneme in the words. Sort the words using the table on the next page. You may want to look up unfamiliar words in a dictionary.

delight   pry   amplify   bite   pie   grind   bonsai   feisty

tie   satellite   environment   frighten   haiku   cycle   comply

almighty   mind   die   kaleidoscope

Dubai   ripe   fortnightly   finally   lie

seismic   twice   Shanghai

OXFORD UNIVERSITY PRESS

igh	
y	
i-e	
ie	
i	
ai	
ei	

2. Choose three words with different letter patterns from the last activity. Write a sentence using each word. Underline the word with the **long /i/** phoneme in each sentence.

a _____

b _____

c _____

1. Write a definition for each homophone. You may use a dictionary to help you.

waist	
waste	

lapse	
laps	

2 Complete the sentences using the correct homophone.

waist   waste   lapse   laps

a Please do not _____ any food.

b I had a _____ of memory and forgot the words of the song.

c I wore a belt around my _____.

d We ran two _____ of the oval.

3 Write a sentence using each homophone.

waist	
waste	
lapse	
laps	

Now try this unit's 'Bringing it together' activity, which your teacher will give you.

OXFORD UNIVERSITY PRESS

UNIT 8

> Some phonemes are voiced and some phonemes are unvoiced.
>
> An example of an unvoiced consonant phoneme is **/sh/** (as in 'shop'). This sound is made using your breath.
>
> An example of a voiced consonant phoneme is **/zh/** (as in 'treasure'). This sound is made using your voice.

Tip

1 Say each word. Can you hear the unvoiced **/sh/** phoneme or the voiced **/zh/** phoneme? Circle the words with a **/sh/** phoneme. Underline the words with a **/zh/** phoneme.

| passionate | measurement | motion | chef | collision |

| astonishment | camouflage | collage | ancient | beige |

2 Say each word and count the syllables.

| astonishment | camouflage | beige | vision |

Sort the words using the table. Then count the phonemes in each word.

	Word	How many phonemes?
One-syllable word		
Two-syllable word		
Three-syllable word		
Four-syllable word		

1 There are many ways to spell the unvoiced **/sh/** phoneme. Find the letter patterns that spell the unvoiced **/sh/** phoneme in the words. Sort the words using the table.

shopping   machine   station   magician   mission   pension

astonishment   motion   chef   passionate   vicious   chauffeur

ancient   traditional   finish   vanish   parachute   specialty

martial   extension   shrubs   mention   controversial

precious   nourish   electrician   dimension   patience

sh	
ch	
si or **ssi**	
ci	
ti	

2 Choose three words from the list in the last activity that you don't write very often. Write a definition for each one. You may use a dictionary to help you.

Word	Definition

> **Tip**
>
> The suffix **-ian** is used to make nouns that describe a person.

1 Read each sentence. Underline the word with the **-ian** suffix. Then circle the matching base word in the sentence.

   a A person who studies mathematics is a mathematician.

   b A person who works with electricity is an electrician.

   c A person who works in a library is a librarian.

   d A person who performs comedy is a comedian.

   e A person who performs music is a musician.

> **Tip**
>
> The suffix **-ion** can be added to the end of some verbs to turn them into nouns. For example, 'action' is a noun made up of the verb 'act' and the suffix **-ion**. 'Action' means the state of acting.

2 Look at the suffixes at the end of each word. Circle the words ending with **-ion**. Underline the words ending with **-ian**.

Tip

Don't forget to use a dictionary to look up any unfamiliar words.

musician   competition   electrician   extension   magician

protection   Australian   composition   librarian   diagnostician

action   promotion   historian

3 Read each sentence. Write the missing verb. Use the noun ending in the suffix **-ion** to help you work out what each verb is. Choose from the base words below.

protect   act   decide   collect

a Scientists wear gloves to _____ themselves from harmful

chemicals. **Protection** from harmful chemicals is needed.

b Fabian and I _____ postage stamps as a hobby. Our stamp

collection includes hundreds of stamps.

c The firefighters need to _____ quickly. Quick **action** by the

firefighters will help to contain the bushfire.

d Our teacher will _____ what our next activity will be.

A **decision** will be made by the teacher.

Now try this unit's 'Bringing it together' activity, which your teacher will give you.

OXFORD UNIVERSITY PRESS

UNIT 9

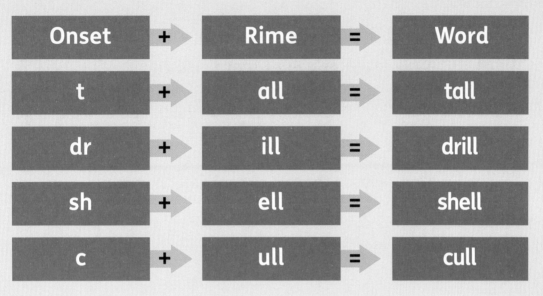

Onset	+	Rime	=	Word
t	+	all	=	tall
dr	+	ill	=	drill
sh	+	ell	=	shell
c	+	ull	=	cull

1 Write words using these onsets and rimes in the table.

Onsets	*f*, *b*, *d*, *t*, *g*, *l*, *m*, *n*, *p*, *s*, *c*, *w*, *y*, *ch*, *sh*, *st*, *dr*, *sm*, *gr*, *sp*, *sk*			
Rimes	*ell* as in 'bell'	*ill* as in 'bill'	*all* or *awl* as in 'ball' or 'bawl'	*ull* as in 'lull'

Focus on the sounds in the rimes. Words ending with the same rime should rhyme, such as 'fall' and 'call'.

Words that end in *ell*, as in 'fell'	Words that end in *ill*, as in 'fill'	Words that end in *all* or *awl*, as in 'fall' or 'bawl'	Words that end in *ull*, as in 'dull'

Ziba Came on a Boat   by Liz Lofthouse

Ziba shivered, and huddled closer to her mother in the crowded hull. Her mother's eyes were full of hope and her lullaby sweet as honey.

2 Read the text above. Find words in the text to complete the table.

One word that...	
has two syllables	
has three syllables	
has four phonemes	
has six phonemes	
starts with a consonant digraph	
starts with a short vowel phoneme	
Two words that...	
end in **ull**	
start with a consonant blend	
have a long vowel phoneme	

OXFORD UNIVERSITY PRESS

1. There are many ways to spell the **/s/** phoneme (as in 'send'). Find the letter patterns involving the **/s/** phoneme in the words. Sort the words using the table.

safety   assess   false   spatial   incident   scientific

psychiatry   castle   city   decrease   fossil   announce

paradise   address   gristle   pseudo   fascinate   commence

circle   wrestle   slump   psalm   promise   decision

muscle   blossom   gust   thistle

s	
ss	
se	
ce	
ci	
sc	
st	
ps	

2. Choose a word from the last activity. Write a short sentence using the word. Underline the word with the **/s/** phoneme.

_____

Adding the suffix **-ment** to the end of a base verb creates a noun that is the result of the action of the verb. 'Payment' is a noun made up of the verb 'pay' and the suffix **-ment**. 'Payment' is the result of paying something.

1 Change each base verb into a noun using the suffix **-ment** to add the missing noun in each sentence. One is done for you.

Base verb	Sentence
refresh	Our coach gave us sliced oranges for <u>refreshment</u>.
manage	Using a diary can help with time _____.
equip	To make our class video, we used a camera and other film _____.

Tip

A morpheme is the smallest meaningful part of a word. 'Jumped' has two meaningful parts: 'jump' and **-ed**.

2 Use an online etymology dictionary to research the origin and meaning of the morpheme **psyche**.

Origin (time and place): _____

Definition:_____

Now use the table below to investigate these words that begin with **psych**.

Root	+ Suffix	= Word	Definition
psych(e)-	-ology		
	-ometrics		

Now try this unit's 'Bringing it together' activity, which your teacher will give you.

OXFORD UNIVERSITY PRESS

UNIT 10

1 Write words using these onsets and rimes.

Onsets	**b**, **f**, **h**, **r**, **j**, **l**, **n**, **w**, **t**, **s**, **ch**, **st**, **br**, **fr**					
Rimes	**alk**, **awk** or **ork** as in 'walk', 'hawk' or 'fork'	**ilk** as in 'silk'	**ulk** as in 'sulk'	**idge** as in 'ridge'	**udge** as in 'fudge'	**edge** as in 'ledge'

Words that end in **alk**, **awk** or **ork**, as in 'talk', 'hawk' or 'fork'	Words that end in **ilk**, as in 'silk'	Words that end in **ulk**, as in 'bulk'

Words that end in **idge**, as in 'ridge'	Words that end in **udge**, as in 'fudge'	Words that end in **edge**, as in 'ledge'

1 Find the words in the word search.

i	o	p	w	b	r	e	a	t	h	e	x	d	j	s
m	a	c	a	m	d	z	c	g	a	g	f	z	l	u
p	g	a	i	s	l	t	r	e	a	s	u	r	e	t
r	a	j	o	r	e	n	d	e	a	v	o	u	r	t
e	i	b	q	u	d	w	r	p	n	v	g	c	b	l
s	n	x	v	v	c	e	m	e	t	e	r	y	e	e
s	s	j	u	u	x	l	e	j	h	j	s	c	c	m
i	t	t	h	r	e	a	t	e	n	e	d	q	k	u
o	f	s	e	t	t	l	e	m	e	n	t	p	o	t
n	i	v	t	y	i	a	y	y	y	i	c	o	n	n

beckon

endeavour

treasure

against

impression

settlement

cemetery

threatened

breath

2 There are a few ways to spell the **short /e/** vowel phoneme. Find the letter patterns that spell the **short /e/** phoneme in the words from the activity at the top of the next page. Sort the words using the chart.

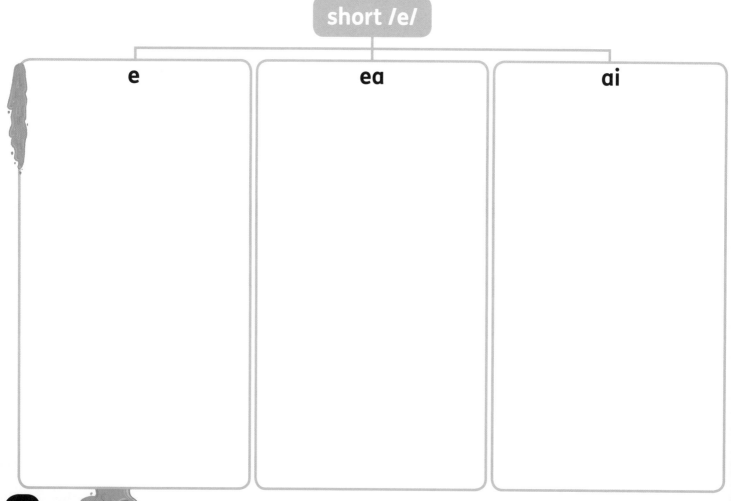

short /e/

e	ea	ai

OXFORD UNIVERSITY PRESS

3 Choose five words from the list that you don't write very often. Write a sentence using each one. You may use a dictionary to help you.

beckon antenna instead jealous dilemma leather again

pleasure impression treasure threatened against method

settlement healthy said cemetery breath chemical

Word	Sentence

1 Use the base verbs in the tables to write sentences using the suffixes **-s**, **-es**, **-ed** and **-ing**. Use the examples to help you.

> **Tip**
>
> When adding suffixes to the base words, remember to use the rules that you have learned so far.

Base verb	Sentence using base verb + suffix **-s** or **-es**
threaten	A robber <u>threatens</u> the shopkeeper.
beckon	
measure	
investigate	
refresh	

Base verb	Sentence using base verb + suffix **-ed**
threaten	A robber <u>threatened</u> the shopkeeper.
beckon	
measure	
investigate	
refresh	

Base verb	Sentence using base verb + suffix **-ing**
threaten	A robber is <u>threatening</u> the shopkeeper.
beckon	
measure	
investigate	
refresh	

Now try this unit's 'Bringing it together' activity, which your teacher will give you.

OXFORD UNIVERSITY PRESS

UNIT 11

Tip

The strongest syllable in a word is the accented syllable. For example, the first syllable of 'teacher' is accented, but the second syllable of 'believe' is accented.

Stolen Girl by Trina Saffiotti

She used to live with her mother in a corrugated iron house with a huge yard that seemed to stretch to the sun. Each morning, they would sit on the verandah eating damper thick with golden syrup and drinking sweet milky tea.

1 Read the text above. Find words from the text to complete the table.

A word that ...	
has four syllables	
starts with a vowel digraph	
has an unaccented final syllable	
rhymes with 'fetch'	
has nine phonemes	
ends with a consonant digraph	
starts with a short vowel phoneme	
starts with a consonant blend	
rhymes with 'kick'	
has a medial long vowel phoneme	

2 Say each word and clap along with the syllables. Underline the vowel letter that represents a schwa in the unaccented syllable. One is done for you.

rock<u>e</u>t rabbit pocket hermit magnet

credit market digit blanket

1 There are many ways to spell the **/j/** phoneme. Find the letter patterns involving the **/j/** phoneme in the words below. Sort the words using the table.

eject pledge legible adjective fragile hedge advantage

enjoyable jokingly baggage sledge gigantic adjacent

porridge bandage imagine injured carriage

j	
dge	
dj	
ge	
gi	

2 Choose two words from the list in the last activity that you don't write very often. Write a definition for each one in the table on the next page.

Word	Definition

Tip

A singular noun is a word for one thing. 'Drum' is a singular noun.

A plural noun is a word that tells us that there is more than one thing. 'Drums' is a plural noun.

The suffix **-s** or **-es** can be added to many nouns to show that there is more than one thing.

1 Use the rules to complete the activities. Add the words to the sentences. Then write your own sentences. Remember to change each base word into a plural noun.

If a base word ends in s, x, z, ch or sh, add the suffix -es.

fox	Several _____ live in the zoo.
paintbrush	

If a base word ends in f or fe, it is usual to change the f or fe to a v and then add the suffix -es.

knife	The butcher sharpens his _____ each day.
life	

If a base word ends in a vowel and the letter _o_, add the suffix -s.

cockatoo	_____ squawk loudly.
video	

If a base word ends in _e_, just add the suffix -s.

resource	Solar and wind are renewable _____ .
beehive	

If a base word ends in a consonant and then _o_, it is usual to add the suffix -es.

echo	We can hear _____ in the tunnel.
dingo	

If a base word ends in a consonant and then _y_, change the _y_ to _i_ and add the suffix -es.

dictionary	Our classroom has many _____ .
community	

Now try this unit's 'Bringing it together' activity, which your teacher will give you.

44

UNIT 12

1 Say each word. Can you hear the different voiced and unvoiced phonemes (**/f/**, **/v/**, unvoiced **/th/** and voiced **/th/**). Sort the words using the table.

| photograph | environmental | threatened | weather | together |

| invasive | demographic | thermometer | clothing | force |

| observation | breath | eighth | breathe | behave |

| friction | length | worthy | volume | different |

/f/ phoneme (unvoiced)	**/v/** phoneme (voiced)

Unvoiced **/th/** phoneme	Voiced **/th/** phoneme

The letter **v** doesn't go by itself at the end of a word. If a word ends with a **/v/** phoneme, it is usually spelled with the letter pattern **ve**.

A word that has a **/v/** phoneme usually has a vowel letter after it. Look at the words 'lava' and 'oven' as examples.

Tip

1 Find the words in the word search.

```
w  q  r  f  r  t  w  d  i  s  s  o  l  v  e  x  x  a  y  z
e  n  d  f  b  c  k  m  j  d  g  p  v  r  h  w  v  n  o  v
b  e  z  n  r  b  z  p  s  h  o  v  e  h  q  u  y  l  e  d
g  g  e  u  a  z  k  v  l  i  v  e  h  a  l  v  e  o  e  s
a  a  r  z  s  l  z  v  c  a  p  t  i  v  e  g  a  v  r  d
v  t  e  a  e  r  o  d  s  c  o  r  r  o  s  i  v  e  g  i
v  i  i  v  e  g  y  w  n  s  b  e  y  j  j  q  f  p  j  a
b  v  i  h  o  s  i  v  r  g  p  e  r  c  e  i  v  e  c  e
c  e  u  d  p  i  r  e  l  a  t  i  v  e  b  v  c  g  g  f
a  l  l  o  i  e  h  x  e  f  f  e  c  t  i  v  e  l  o  p
b  e  a  v  v  v  d  d  g  h  a  v  e  u  o  u  k  o  v  e
c  e  v  j  e  e  d  w  b  b  r  r  j  m  n  g  z  v  a  r
d  b  i  t  e  d  o  v  e  n  q  c  r  p  y  l  h  e  d  e
p  a  n  n  x  q  a  r  i  x  l  n  e  r  v  e  u  x  b  v
s  v  o  y  q  t  j  h  f  o  r  g  i  v  e  d  y  c  s  a
```

halve

live

captive

have

dissolve

shove

nerve

dove

relative

glove

forgive

corrosive

sieve

love

effective

perceive

negative

2 Read out loud from a book you are reading in class. Find three words with a **/v/** phoneme. Write the words in the table, along with the sentences you found them in. Then, in each word you wrote in the left column, underline the letter **v** and the vowel letter that comes after it.

Word with **/v/** phoneme	Sentence from your book

Tip

The suffix **-er** can change a base verb to a person noun. For example, the verb 'teach' can be changed to the noun 'teacher'. 'Teacher' means a person who teaches.

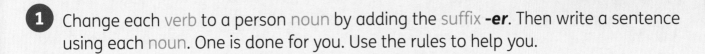

Morphology

1 Change each verb to a person noun by adding the suffix **-er**. Then write a sentence using each noun. One is done for you. Use the rules to help you.

Verb	Person noun + suffix **-er**	Sentence
teach	teacher	A person who teaches students is a <u>teacher</u>.
photograph		
clean		

If the base word ends in e, drop the e and then add the suffix -er.

Verb	Person noun + suffix *-er*	Sentence
bake	baker	A person who bakes bread is a <u>baker</u>.
dance		
write		

If the base word ends with a short vowel graph then a consonant graph, double the last letter and add the suffix -er.

Verb	Person noun + suffix *-er*	Sentence
run	runner	A person who runs is a <u>runner</u>.
blog		
drum		

Now try this unit's 'Bringing it together' activity, which your teacher will give you.

UNIT 13

Tip

> A diphthong is a kind of long vowel sound that you make by moving your mouth in two ways. For example, the phonemes **/ow/**, as in 'cow', **/oi/**, as in 'boy', and **long /a/**, as in 'spray', are also diphthongs.

1   Say each word. Can you hear the diphthongs? Sort the words using the table.

| fountain | avoid | survey | convoy | aloud | display |

| pointing | surround | array | loyal | claiming | empower |

Words with **/ow/** phoneme	Words with **/oi/** phoneme	Words with the **long /a/** phoneme

2   Find words from a book you are reading to complete the table.

A word that ...	
has three syllables	
has four syllables	
has four phonemes	
has seven phonemes	

starts with a vowel digraph	
has an unaccented final syllable	
has the **/ow/** phoneme	
has the **/oi/** phoneme	
has the **long /a/** phoneme	
starts or ends with a consonant digraph	
starts with a short vowel phoneme	
has a medial long vowel phoneme	

1 Write these words in alphabetical order.

destroy   deploy   discount   disappointing   downwards

1 _____

2 _____

3 _____

4 _____

5 _____

2 Look at the letter patterns that represent diphthongs in the words. Sort the words using the table. Then underline the letter patterns for diphthongs in each word.

point   brown   voice   deploy   tower   mountain

announce   avoiding   royal   disappointing   moisture

destroy   voyage   loudest   employ   proud   downwards

discount   showering   powerful

Words with **ow**	Words with **ou**

Words with **oy**	Words with **oi**

An adjective is a word that describes something. 'Tall' is an adjective.

The suffix **-er** can be added to adjectives to compare things. The suffix **-er** is a comparative suffix.

This is a tall box.

This box is taller.

Tip

Morphology

1 Read the adjectives. Add the suffix **-er** to each one. Use the rules to help you.

hard: harder   small: _____   short: _____

> **If the base word ends in e, drop the e and then add the suffix -er.**

close: closer   wise: _____

> **If the base word ends with a short vowel graph then a consonant graph, double the last letter and add the suffix -er.**

fit: fitter   hot: _____

> **If the base word ends with a consonant and then y, change the y to i and add the suffix -er.**

shiny: shinier   bumpy: _____

2 Write the missing word in the sentence below. Then choose two other base words from the last activity and write a sentence for each one. Remember to add the suffix **-er** to each base word.

Base word	Sentence
shiny	The polished rock was _____ than the unpolished rock.

> **Now try this unit's 'Bringing it together' activity, which your teacher will give you.**

OXFORD UNIVERSITY PRESS

1 Say each word. Listen for the rimes at the end of each word. Circle the words with the same rime as 'sort'. Underline the words with the same rime as 'light'.

| taught | flight | delight | bought | caught | fright |

| despite | thought | height | brought | ignite | distraught |

2 Count the phonemes in the words from the last activity. Write a word in each box.

A word with three phonemes	
A word with four phonemes	
A word with five phonemes	
A word with six phonemes	
A word with seven phonemes	

1 Write these homophones in alphabetical order.

| soar | sore | bored | pour | saw | poor | board | paw |

1 _____   2 _____

3 _____   4 _____

5 _____   6 _____

7 _____   8 _____

2 There are many ways to spell the **/aw/** phoneme (as in the word 'fork'). Find the letter patterns involving the **/aw/** phoneme in the words. Sort the words using the table.

normal   fawn   author   stalk   award   soar   moor   ignore

pour   sought   awful   small   board   brought   carnivore   court

absorb   applaud   swarm   floor   thought   explore   hoarse

drawn   launch   corner   quarter   poor   gourmet

or	
aw	
au	
al or **all**	
ar	
oar	
oor	
ore	
our	
ough	

The suffix **-est**, meaning 'most', can be added to the end of a base word. This suffix is called a superlative suffix.

Tip

The gorilla is tall.

The zebra is taller.

The giraffe is tallest.

1 Add the superlative suffix **-est** to the end of each base word. Use the rules to help you.

loud: loudest   rough: _____

If the base word ends in e, drop the e and then add the suffix -est.

close: closest   wise: _____

If the base word ends with a short vowel graph then a consonant graph, double the last letter and add the suffix -est.

fit: fittest   thin: _____

If the base word ends in a consonant and then y, change the y to i and add the suffix -est.

shiny: shiniest   bumpy: _____

2 Add the superlative suffix **-est** to each of the base words. Then write a sentence using the words with suffixes. One has been started for you.

loud	loudest	The trumpet was the _____.
close		
fit		
shiny		

3 Complete the sentences using the correct homophone.

horse	hoarse	saw	sore	soar

pour	poor	more	moor	board	bored

a The hawk will _____ into the sky.

b Please _____ the milk into the jug.

c I would like to walk in the rainforest _____ often.

d His voice was _____ after all his cheering.

e The boat will _____ alongside the dock.

f The opposite of being _____ is being entertained.

g Serika's muscles were feeling _____ after the triathlon.

h The old car is in _____ condition.

i The rider fell off the _____ when it stumbled.

j It has been two years since we last _____ each other.

k Chess is played on a _____ with black and white squares.

Now try this unit's 'Bringing it together' activity, which your teacher will give you.

OXFORD UNIVERSITY PRESS

UNIT 15

> **Tip**
> In some words, when a vowel is followed by the letter **r**, it changes the way the vowel sounds. This is called an r-influenced vowel phoneme.

1 These words have an r-influenced vowel phoneme. Sort the words using the table.

| nervous | hair | startle | heritage | mermaid | stark |

| hearty | rehearse | scariest | prepare | learn | canary |

| declare | arch | compare | earth | research | charming |

| beware | sharpest | disturb | curve | hardest | charred |

/er/ as in 'her'	**/air/** as in 'chair'	**/ar/** as in 'dark'

2 Look in a book you are reading. Add some more words from your book to the table above.

1 There are many ways to spell the **/er/** phoneme. Find the letter patterns that spell the **/er/** phoneme in the words. Sort the words using the table.

| first | person | research | burn | structures | worst | journal |

| theatre | metre | worship | churn | yearn | journey | concern |

| mermaid | manufactures | nocturnal | worth |

| creature | early | dirty | litre | courtesy |

ir	er	ear	ur

ure	or	our	re

> **Tip**
> Sometimes these letter patterns can be pronounced differently, depending on the accent or dialect of the person speaking. Sometimes these letter patterns can be pronounced as a schwa, an **/uh/** sound, but the spelling doesn't change.

2 Look in a book you are reading. Add more words from your book to the table above.

Things That Are Most in the World
by Judi Barrett

The teensy-weensiest thing in the world is a newborn flea.

1 Write a creative sentence for each base word. Each sentence must use the base word with a comparative suffix (**-er**) and the base word with a superlative suffix (**-est**). Underline the words with suffixes you have used in each sentence. Use the sentence above and the example below to help you.

Base word	Sentence
long	*A bus is <u>longer</u> than a car but the <u>longest</u> thing in the world is every single strand of spaghetti tied together end to end.*
smelly	
wide	
cool	
short	

Now try this unit's 'Bringing it together' activity, which your teacher will give you.

UNIT 16

1 These words have an r-influenced vowel phoneme. Sort the words using the table.

startle   heritage   nervous   support   research

aerial   steer   appear   prepare   award   confirm

calendar   engineer   collar   shortest

/ear/ as in 'near'	
/ar/ as in 'start'	
/air/ as in 'chair'	
/er/ as in 'her'	
/aw/ as in 'form'	

Tip

Sometimes the **/er/** or **/ar/** phonemes can sound a little different, depending on the way a person pronounces them. Sometimes they can sound like a schwa, an **/uh/** sound, but the spelling doesn't change.

2 Look in a book you are reading in class. Find some more words with an r-influenced vowel phoneme, like those in the last activity. Add them into the table above.

OXFORD UNIVERSITY PRESS

1 There are many ways to spell the **/k/** phoneme. Find the letter patterns that spell the **/k/** phoneme in the words. Sort the words using the table.

colour   koala   chopsticks   technology   plaque   silk

athletics   magical   pumpkin   echidna   opaque   kilometre

chameleon   attack   antique   chaos   musical   boutique

fantastic   humpback   kidney   bucket   psychology

c	
k	
ck	
ch	
que	

2 Choose three words from the list in the last activity that you don't write very often. Write a definition for each one.

Word	Definition

The suffixes **-able** and **-ible** can be added to the end of a word to form an adjective. These suffixes mean 'able to be' or 'worthy of'.

The picnic in the park was enjoy**able**. The picnic was **able to be** enjoyed.

The suffix **-able** is more common than the suffix **-ible**.

The suffix **-able** is usually added to a complete word. But, if a word ends in the **/s/** phoneme, it is common to use **-ible** instead. The suffix **-ible** is also commonly used after an incomplete word.

1 Add the suffix **-able** to each of the base words. Then write a sentence using each adjective you have made. Underline the adjective in each sentence. One is done for you.

Base word	Adjective + suffix **-able**	Sentence
enjoy	enjoyable	It was an <u>enjoyable</u> picnic.
manage		
agree		
comfort		

2 The adjectives in the table on the next page end with the suffix **-ible**. Underline the suffix **-ible** in each word. Then write the base word that each adjective comes from. Notice that these base words end in the **/s/** phoneme. Write a sentence using each adjective.

If the base word ends in e, usually drop the e and then add the suffix -ible.

OXFORD UNIVERSITY PRESS

Adjective + suffix *-ible*	Base word	Sentence
revers<u>ible</u>	reverse	Melting and freezing are examples of reversible changes.
flexible		
sensible		

3 Read the adjectives. Notice that these words also end in the *-ible* suffix, but the letters that come before this suffix do not make a complete word. Underline the suffix in each adjective. Circle the part of the word that comes before the suffix. Then use each adjective in a sentence. One is done for you.

Adjective + suffix *-ible*	Sentence
(vis)<u>ible</u>	The blue sky is visible through the window.
horrible	
audible	
edible	

Now try this unit's 'Bringing it together' activity, which your teacher will give you.

Tip

A multisyllabic word has more than one syllable. 'Apple' and 'scientist' are both multisyllabic words.

Pencil of Doom   by Andy Griffiths

The presentation was to be held that evening in the town square. The winner got a framed certificate and one hundred dollars in prize money.

1 Read the text above. Find words in the text to complete the table.

Two four-syllable words	
Two words with a **long** /a/ vowel phoneme	
Two words with a **short** /a/ vowel phoneme	
Two words with an unaccented final syllable	
A word with four phonemes	
A word with five phonemes	
Two words that start with a consonant blend	
Two words with a schwa	

OXFORD UNIVERSITY PRESS

2 Look in a book you are reading in class. Find some multisyllabic words with a **short /a/** phoneme and some multisyllabic words with a **long /a/** phoneme. Write these words in the table. Use the examples to help you.

Short /a/ phoneme	Long /a/ phoneme
trampoline	chamber

1 Choose four words from the list on the next page that you don't write very often. Write a definition for each one. You may use a dictionary to help you.

Word	Definition

2 There are many ways to spell the **long /a/** phoneme. Find the letter patterns that spell the **long /a/** phoneme. Sort the words using the table.

activate   acclaim   display   freight   obey   vein   break

sleigh   calculate   delay   contain   neighbour   survey

veil   great   sundae   convey   explain   decorate

steak   weight   indicate   sustainability   pathway

beige   straying   vertebrae   prey   reggae   apron

ay	
ai	
a-e	
ei	
eigh	
a	
ae	
ey	
ea	

3 Write these homophones in alphabetical order.

| reign | prey | whey | rein | weigh | rain | way | pray |

1 _____   2 _____

3 _____   4 _____

5 _____   6 _____

7 _____   8 _____

1 Complete the sentences using the correct homophone.

| way | weigh | whey | prey |

| pray | rein | reign | rain |

a We need to _____ each ingredient when baking a cake.

b We have a long _____ to go before we reach our destination.

c A rider uses a _____ to guide the horse.

d A hungry eagle circled above looking for _____.

e A milk product that can be used to make cheese is _____.

f The weather bureau predicts _____ for most of the day.

g A church is a place where people can go to _____.

h The king was a popular ruler throughout his _____.

> **Now try this unit's 'Bringing it together' activity, which your teacher will give you.**

Pencil of Doom
by Andy Griffith

Jack was sympathetic, but still refused to believe that our injuries were due to anything more than coincidence.

1 Read the text above. Find words in the text to complete the table.

Two two-syllable words	
Two three-syllable words	
Two four-syllable words	
A word with a **short /e/** vowel phoneme	
A word with a **long /e/** vowel phoneme	
Two words with an accented final syllable	
Three words that end with a consonant digraph	
Two words with ten phonemes	

OXFORD UNIVERSITY PRESS

2 Look in a book you are reading in class. Find some multisyllabic words with a **short /e/** phoneme, and some multisyllabic words with a **long /e/** phoneme. Write the words in the table.

Short /e/ phoneme	Long /e/ phoneme
c<u>e</u>ntury	b<u>ea</u>con

1 There are many ways to spell the **long /e/** phoneme. Find the letter patterns that spell the **long /e/** phoneme in the words. Sort the words using the table.

team   centipede   chief   receive   field   fever   degree

ceiling   reaching   delete   yield   protein   referee

seamless   museum   deepest   recent   relief   Japanese

ee	
ea	
ei	
e	
ie	
e-e	

2 Find the words in the word search.

c	h	i	e	f	v	m	y	m	e	m	u	s	y	u
q	n	e	m	d	h	y	f	i	e	l	d	m	p	a
c	p	p	p	d	r	f	r	e	c	e	i	v	e	a
e	p	e	m	u	s	e	u	m	a	p	r	o	k	m
i	r	x	z	g	g	e	y	d	e	l	e	t	e	u
l	o	t	r	e	f	e	r	e	e	v	f	g	l	y
i	t	r	c	e	n	t	i	p	e	d	e	f	u	a
n	e	a	r	e	l	i	e	f	i	i	d	k	g	f
g	i	n	m	n	h	s	e	i	z	e	z	c	t	a
t	n	e	e	x	t	r	e	m	e	u	j	a	i	b

emu   protein

centipede   referee

chief   extreme

receive   museum

field   seize

ceiling   relief

delete

Tip

The suffix **-less** means 'without' or 'lacking in'. 'Careless' is an adjective made from the noun 'care' and the suffix **-less**. It means 'without care'.

Morphology

1 Complete the table by adding the suffix **-less** to each base word. Then write the meaning of each new word. One is done for you.

Base word	Adjective + suffix **-less**	Meaning
care	careless	without care
flight		
tooth		
fear		
taste		

OXFORD UNIVERSITY PRESS

Base word	Adjective + suffix **-less**	Meaning
power		
breath		
thought		

2 Choose any four of the words with suffixes from the last activity. Write a sentence using each one. Underline the word with a suffix in each sentence. Two examples are provided.

Word ending in suffix **-less**	Sentence
careless	I made some <u>careless</u> mistakes in my project.
flightless	Emus and ostriches are <u>flightless</u> birds.

Now try this unit's 'Bringing it together' activity, which your teacher will give you.

Pencil of Doom
by Andy Griffiths

Smoke started pouring out of the bottom of it. Bits started falling off. First, buttons, then handles, then, to our astonishment, whole panels!

1 Read the text above. Find words from the text to complete the table.

Three words that end with a consonant blend	
A four-syllable word	
Four words with a **short /o/** vowel phoneme	
A word with a **long /o/** vowel phoneme	
Four words with an unaccented final syllable	
Two words that start with a consonant blend	
Two words that start with a consonant digraph	

OXFORD UNIVERSITY PRESS

2 Look in a book you are reading in class. Find some multisyllabic words with a **short /o/** phoneme (as in the word 'shot'), and some multisyllabic words with a **long /o/** phoneme (as in the word 'boat'). Write the words in the table.

Short /o/ phoneme as in 'shot'	Long /o/ phoneme as in 'boat'
d<u>o</u>ctor	arr<u>ow</u>

1 Find the words in the word search.

w	c	s	a	b	v	n	k	l	c	v	o	t	e	x
k	b	p	l	a	t	e	a	u	b	u	r	e	a	u
x	l	i	b	t	v	e	p	i	s	o	d	e	x	s
i	o	l	s	a	d	d	i	a	g	n	o	s	e	e
k	a	w	b	e	l	l	o	w	f	e	j	z	s	n
t	t	a	n	o	t	i	c	e	n	t	z	w	o	e
a	a	l	t	h	o	u	g	h	e	i	m	j	k	i
b	o	n	u	s	o	w	r	p	y	c	x	r	o	e
d	n	c	e	l	o	a	t	h	r	e	g	x	i	j
c	o	r	r	o	d	e	w	g	s	f	m	o	a	t

bellow   roe

diagnose   bureau

bonus   loath

woe   vote

plateau   although

corrode   notice

moat   episode

Orthography

2 There are many ways to spell the **long /o/** phoneme (as in the word 'boat'). Find the letter patterns that spell the **long /o/** phoneme in the words. Sort the words using the table.

| bloated | bellowing | diagnose | bonus | woeful | dough |

| plateau | locally | corrode | moat | swallowing | roe | bureau |

| though | loath | vote | bistro | mellow | although | croak |

| gateau | noticing | episode | bestow | soaking | aloe |

oa	
ow	
o-e	
o	
oe	
ough	
eau	

OXFORD UNIVERSITY PRESS

1 Complete the sentences using the correct homophone. You may use a dictionary to help you.

where	wear	we're

a I suggest you _____ a warm coat today.

b We need a map to find out _____ to go.

c While _____ at the beach, we can play a game of cricket.

d On the holidays, _____ did you go?

e I _____ a helmet while riding my bike.

f My friends and I are going swimming because _____ feeling hot.

2 Write a definition for each homophone.

where	
we're	
wear	

3 Write a sentence using each homophone.

where	
wear	
we're	

Now try this unit's 'Bringing it together' activity, which your teacher will give you.

Withering-by-Sea
by Judith Rossell

Stella Montgomery lay hidden behind the ferns in the conservatory of the Hotel Majestic, flat on the mossy tiles, tracing a path through the Amazon jungle in a small, damp atlas.

1 Read the text above. Find words from the text to complete the table.

A one-syllable word with a **short /o/** vowel phoneme	
A two-syllable word with a **short /o/** vowel phoneme	
A four-syllable word with a **short /o/** vowel phoneme	
A two-syllable word with a **long /o/** vowel phoneme	
All three-syllable words you can find	
Three one-syllable words that start with a consonant blend	
A word that rhymes with 'grew'	

OXFORD UNIVERSITY PRESS

2 Look in a book you are reading in class. Find some multisyllabic words with a **short /o/** phoneme (as in 'dot'), and some multisyllabic words with a **short /oo/** phoneme (as in 'took'). Write the words in the table.

Short /o/ phoneme as in 'dot'	Short /oo/ phoneme as in 'took'
m<u>o</u>dern	b<u>oo</u>klet

1 Find the words in the word search.

h	f	u	g	f	l	e	b	y	u	c	b	g	a	j
l	e	g	r	u	e	s	o	m	e	d	g	x	y	e
a	w	m	v	w	a	n	z	o	l	n	b	h	v	w
g	s	c	e	v	c	x	z	v	s	i	w	b	s	e
o	o	o	c	e	j	p	o	l	l	u	t	e	e	l
o	z	c	l	u	e	t	h	r	o	u	g	h	w	l
n	s	a	b	s	o	l	u	t	e	i	h	u	e	e
c	q	d	i	s	a	p	p	r	o	v	e	a	r	r
j	c	o	u	r	i	e	r	d	c	e	k	q	t	y
h	b	n	t	e	t	o	h	r	e	c	r	u	i	t

clue

lagoon

through

absolute

recruit

jewellery

disapprove

sewer

gruesome

pollute

courier

2 There are many ways to spell the **long /oo/** phoneme (as in 'boot'). Find the letter patterns that spell the **long /oo/** phoneme in the words. Sort the words using the table.

clue   lagoon   throughout   remove   absolute   juicy

super   recruit   youthful   jewellery   disapprove   lunar

sewer   gruesome   pollute   pontoon   coupon

ue	
oo	
u-e	
ew	
ou	
u	
ui	
o	
ough	

OXFORD UNIVERSITY PRESS

3 Choose two words from the last activity. Write them in a sentence.

_____

_____

1 Complete the sentences using the correct homophone. You may use a dictionary to help you.

| through | threw | blew | blue |

a I sneezed and _____ my nose.

b The toddler _____ a toy across the room.

c The colour of the sea is navy _____.

d A spider crawled _____ the damp pipe.

2 Write a sentence using each homophone.

through	
threw	
blew	
blue	

Now try this unit's 'Bringing it together' activity, which your teacher will give you.

Withering-by-Sea   by Judith Rossell

The drip and trickle of water and the hiss of steam under the grating in the floor seemed to mingle with the swish of jungle trees in the wind and the screams of parrots.

1 Read the text above. Find words from the text to complete the table.

All one-syllable words with a medial **short /i/** vowel phoneme	
All two-syllable words with a **short /i/** vowel phoneme	
All words with a **long /e/** vowel phoneme	
All words with an unaccented final syllable and **/l/** as the final phoneme	
A four-phoneme word	
A six-phoneme word	
Two words that start with a consonant blend and end with a consonant digraph	

OXFORD UNIVERSITY PRESS

2 Look in a book you are reading in class. Find some multisyllabic words with a **short /i/** phoneme, and some multisyllabic words with a **long /i/** phoneme. Write the words in the table.

Short /i/ phoneme	Long /i/ phoneme
triplet	migrant

1 Choose three words from the list in the activity on the next page that you do not write very often. Write a definition for each one.

Word	Definition

2 There are many ways to spell the **long /i/** phoneme. Find the letter patterns that spell the **long /i/** phoneme in the words. Sort the words using the table.

delightful   prying   quite   lie   crisis   bonsai   seismograph

environment   haiku   pie   amplify   satellite   frightened

enlighten   migrant   recycling   shine   feisty

slightly   kaleidoscope   library   Thailand

magnify   divide   tie

Tip

Don't forget to use a dictionary to help you with unfamiliar words.

igh	
y	
i-e	
ie	
i	
ai	
ei	

OXFORD UNIVERSITY PRESS

1 Complete the sentences using the correct homophone: 'night' or 'knight', and 'sight' or 'site'. You may use a dictionary to help you.

a The concert will be held at a different _____ next month.

b The opposite of day is _____.

2 Write a sentence using each homophone.

knight	
sight	

Tip

The suffix **-ful** changes a noun to an adjective. It means 'full of'. 'Doubtful' is an adjective that means 'full of doubt'.

3 Complete the sentences by adding an adjective that ends with the suffix **-ful**. Use the bold words as a clue.

a Prisha **helped** to pack boxes. She was being _____.

b The decoration has many **colours**. The decoration is _____.

c The children were **cheering** up. The children became _____.

d Please **respect** each other. We were asked to be _____.

4 Write your own sentence using adjectives that end in the suffix **-ful**. If you're not sure, try using one of these base words to get started: 'power', 'pain', 'thought' or 'hope'.

_____

Now try this unit's 'Bringing it together' activity, which your teacher will give you.

UNIT 22

1 Write words using these onsets and rimes.

Onsets	*r, l, f, m, d, tw, pl, gr, tr, pr, sp*	
Rimes	*ice* as in 'rice'	*ace* as in 'race'

Words that end in *ice*, as in 'rice'	Words that end in *ace*, as in 'race'

> **Tip**
>
> A disyllabic word **contains two** syllables. 'Rabbit' is a disyllabic word.

2 Say each word while clapping along with the syllables. Notice that each word is disyllabic. In some of the words, the first syllable is accented (the beat feels stronger). For the other words, the second syllable is accented. Circle the words with an accented first syllable.

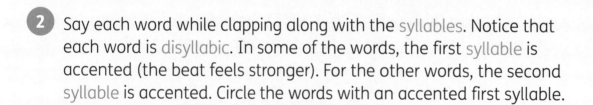

angle	divide	cycle	equal	predict	array	liquid

supply	dial	ripple	reply	water	undone	delay

OXFORD UNIVERSITY PRESS

1 Each word listed below is missing its second syllable. Complete each word by adding **le** or **al** to form a final unaccented syllable. You may use a dictionary to help you.

bott_____   ripp_____   ment_____

loc_____   mor_____   cast_____

thrott_____   ped_____   midd_____

jung_____   equ_____

2 Sort the words from the last activity using the table.

Words that end in **le**	Words that end in **al**

Tip

Many adjectives can be changed to nouns by adding the suffix **-ness**. 'Coldness' is made up of the adjective 'cold' and the suffix **-ness**. 'Coldness' means 'the state of being cold'.

Adjective	+ Suffix	= Noun	Meaning of noun	Used in a sentence
happy	ness	happiness	The state of being happy	I wish you happiness.

> **If the base adjective ends in _y_, usually change the _y_ to _i_ before adding the suffix _-ness_.   happy | happiness**

1 Complete the table by changing each adjective to a noun using the suffix **-ness**. Then write the meaning of each noun. One is done for you.

Adjective	Noun	Meaning of noun
tidy	tidiness	the state of being tidy
soft		
weak		
nervous		
forgetful		
thoughtful		
sick		
lazy		
fit		
empty		
thick		

Now try this unit's 'Bringing it together' activity, which your teacher will give you.

OXFORD UNIVERSITY PRESS

UNIT 23

> **Tip**
>
> Alliteration is when a group of words that are close together start with the same sound or sounds. Here is an example.
>
> ***St**rangely, **strong str**ing beans **str**enuously **str**angle **str**ipy **str**awberry **str**udels.*

1 Write a sentence that shows alliteration using any of these words. You may add suffixes to the words if you need to.

strange	stride	straw	strum	stripe	stream	straight

street	strive	struggle	strong	stretch	strawberry

strenuous	stranded	strength	string	strudel	structure

_____

_____

2 Count the syllables in each word. Then sort each word using the table and count the phonemes.

structurally	strong	strawberry	struggle

	Word	How many phonemes?
One-syllable word		
Two-syllable word		
Three-syllable word		
Four-syllable word		

1 Read each base word. Notice the letter patterns in the unaccented final syllable. Sort the words into the column of the table that matches the letter pattern at the end of each word.

doctor   flavour   sister   collar   pillar

summer   anchor   colour   author   polar

armour   factor   corner   grammar   answer

harbour   dollar   mirror   fever   humour

Words that end in **or**	
Words that end in **our**	
Words that end in **er**	
Words that end in **ar**	

1 Complete the sentences in the table on the next page by writing the missing verb related to the base word. Each missing verb needs a suffix that shows tense: **-ed** or **-ing**.

Tip

If you need to check the rules for using the suffix **-ing**, refer to pages 15–16.

If you need to check the rules for using the suffix **-ed**, refer to pages 23–24.

The Shaggy Gully Times
by Jackie French

Base word	Sentence
decide	I _____ it couldn't be too hard.
unlock	Gertie _____ her cage.
save	We _____ the animals!
look	I can't thank the lyrebird family enough for _____ after me.
pop	We had just _____ out for a night at the ballet.
fly	It wasn't easy _____ a plane.
rescue	Shaggy Gully residents put forward many ideas for _____ the animals.

2 For each word in the table, explain a spelling rule that was followed to add the suffix to the base verb. One is done for you.

escaped	If a word ends in **e**, drop the **e** before adding the suffix **-ed**.
tapping	
carried	
landing	
rushed	

Now try this unit's 'Bringing it together' activity, which your teacher will give you.

UNIT 24

1 Read each word. In the top row of the table, write the letter patterns used to represent the initial consonant blends. Then sort the words using the table.

| shrill | scramble | stretch | sprout | shrink | shroud | scratch |

| spread | sprawl | strand | shrimp | screech | strange | sprain |

| sprinkle | shrug | stream | scrounge | straight | scribble |

Initial consonant blend: **shr**	Initial consonant blend: _____	Initial consonant blend: _____	Initial consonant blend: _____
shrill			

2 Count the syllables in each word. Then sort the words using the table and count the phonemes.

| scramble | straight | spreadable |

	Word	How many phonemes?
One-syllable word		
Two-syllable word		
Three-syllable word		

OXFORD UNIVERSITY PRESS

Tip

If the first syllable of a disyllabic word has a short vowel graph followed by one consonant letter, it is common for the medial consonant letter to be doubled. This is called a medial consonant doublet. In the word 'shuttle', **u** is a short vowel graph, and the letters **tt** make a medial consonant doublet.

1 Write the missing consonant letter in these disyllabic words. Say each word and clap along with the syllables. Circle the letter that represents the short vowel in the first syllable of each word. One has been done for you.

sh(u)ttle   drib____le   dab____le   mam____al

of____ice   wad____le   bot____le   mid____le

hob____le   hap____y   pad____le   pil____ow

ap____le   chal____enge   pup____y   hap____en

2 Some of these words have a medial consonant doublet. Sort the words.

| sample | giggle | cradle | gurgle | bottle | window | cashew | middle |

| pillow | angel | donate | happy | mammal | open | challenge | happen |

Medial consonant is doubled	Medial consonant is not doubled

3 Look again at the words from the last activity. When do you think a medial consonant is **not** doubled?

_____

_____

The suffix **-ion** can be added to some nouns to make verbs.

If the base verb ends in *d*, *de* or *se*, replace these letters with *s* and then add the suffix *-ion*.

1 Read each verb. Underline the letter or letters that spell the **last** phoneme. Then change each verb to a noun by adding the suffix **-ion**.

Base verb	Noun + *-ion* suffix	Base verb	Noun + *-ion* suffix
conclu**de**	conclusion	comprehend	
collide		extend	
erode		include	
divide		persuade	
explode		provide	
invade		revise	
corrode		confuse	
decide		discuss	
exclude		progress	

Now try this unit's 'Bringing it together' activity, which your teacher will give you.

OXFORD UNIVERSITY PRESS

UNIT 25

Withering-by-Sea
by Judith Rossell

It looked large enough to swallow an elephant and had a hungry expression.

1 Read the text above. Find words from the text to complete the table.

All of the one-syllable words starting with a consonant	
All of the two-syllable words	
All of the three-syllable words	
A four-phoneme word	
A five-phoneme word	
Two words with a schwa in the final syllable	
A seven-phoneme word	
The two-syllable words with an unaccented final syllable	

2 Write words using these onsets and rimes.

Onsets	b, m, g, h, r, wr, c, s, sl, fl, bl, dr, thr, kn, n, sh		
Rimes	**oat** or **ote** as in 'goat' or 'wrote'	**oap** or **ope** as in 'soap' or 'hope'	**oan, own, ewn** or **one** as in 'groan', 'grown', 'sewn' or 'bone'

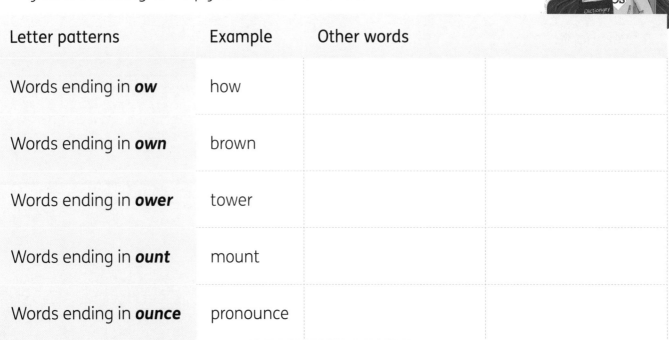

Words that end in **oat** or **ote**	Words that end in **ope** or **oap**	Words that end in **oan, own, ewn** or **one**

1 Complete the table by writing words with the diphthong **/ow/**, as in 'how' and 'loud'. You may use a dictionary or a book you are reading to help you find some words.

Letter patterns	Example	Other words	
Words ending in **ow**	how		
Words ending in **own**	brown		
Words ending in **ower**	tower		
Words ending in **ount**	mount		
Words ending in **ounce**	pronounce		

Letter patterns	Example	Other words	
Words ending in **ouse**	rouse		
Words ending in **oud**	loud		
Words ending in **ound**	found		

2) Look again at the words in the table from the last activity. Underline the **ow** digraphs. Circle the **ou** digraphs.

Use the sentence starters to write your ideas about when to use these digraphs.

I can use **ow** when ...

I can use **ou** when ...

Tip

The suffix **-ion** changes a verb into a noun.

1) Use the rules to change verbs into nouns with the suffix **-ion**. Use the examples to help you.

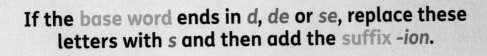

If the base word ends in *d*, *de* or *se*, replace these letters with *s* and then add the suffix *-ion*.

Verb	divide	explode		collide
Noun	division			

Verb	correct	attract	collect
Noun	correction		

Verb	permit	admit	emit
Noun	permission		

Verb	educate	communicate	celebrate
Noun	education		

Verb	describe	prescribe	transcribe
Noun	description		

Now try this unit's 'Bringing
it together' activity, which your
teacher will give you.

96

UNIT 26

1 Write a sentence that shows alliteration using any of these words. You may add suffixes if you need to.

shrink	shroud	shrimp	shrug	shriek	shrivel

shrewd	shrine	shrub	shrill	shrubbery	shred

_____

_____

2 Count the syllables in each word. Then sort the words using the table and count the phonemes.

shrubbery	shrub	shrouded	shrugged	shrivel	shrinkable

	Word	How many phonemes?
One-syllable words		
Two-syllable words		
Three-syllable words		

1 Complete the table by writing words with the diphthong
/oi/, as in 'coy' and 'coin'. You may use a dictionary or a
book you are reading to help you find some words.

Letter patterns	Example	Other words	
Words ending in **oy**	coy		
Words with **oy** in the initial accented syllable	voyage		
Words ending in **oin**	loin		
Words ending in **oice**	rejoice		
Words with **oi** and ending in **t**	moist		
Words ending in **oil**	toil		

2 Look again at the words you wrote in the last activity. Underline the **oy** digraphs.
Circle the **oi** digraphs.

3 Use the sentence starters to help you write your ideas about how to spell this sound.

I can use **oy** when ...

I can use **oi** when ...

OXFORD UNIVERSITY PRESS

Tip

A free morpheme is a meaningful part of a word that is also a complete word on its own. In the word 'preschool', **school** is a free morpheme.

A bound morpheme is a meaningful part of a word that cannot make a word on its own. In the word 'preschool', **pre** is a bound morpheme. It has its own meaning ('before'), but it is not a word by itself.

A prefix is a bound morpheme that can be added before another morpheme to make a new word. **Uni-** is a prefix that means 'one'.

Free morphemes (base words)		Bound morphemes (units of meaning that are not complete words)	
cycle	form	ped	ruple
angle	verse	athlon	agon
corn	plane	ceratops	acle
graph	pod	plet	ple

1 Use the morphemes in the table above to create words that start with the prefixes shown below. Create as many new words as you can. You may use a dictionary to help you. An example and meaning for each prefix is provided.

Prefix: *uni-*	Prefix: *bi-*	Prefix: *tri-*	Prefix: *quad-*	Prefix: *pent-*
Meaning: 'one'	Meaning: 'two'	Meaning: 'three'	Meaning: 'four'	Meaning: 'five'
unicycle	bicycle	tricycle	quadgraph	pentagon

Now try this unit's 'Bringing it together' activity, which your teacher will give you.

1 Write a sentence that shows alliteration using any of these words. You may add suffixes to the words if you need to.

| force | friction | feather | fire | phenomena | forward |

| fraction | fear | ferocious | flame | fly | flamingo |

| flop | favourite | feature | festival | follow | flounder |

_____

_____

2 Count the syllables in each word. Then sort the words using the table and count the phonemes.

| phenomena | friction | ferociously | flammable | fractional | finding |

	Word	How many phonemes?
Two-syllable words		
Three-syllable words		
Four-syllable words		

OXFORD UNIVERSITY PRESS

1 There are many ways to spell the **/f/** phoneme. Find the letter patterns that spell the **/f/** phoneme in the words. Sort the words using the chart.

ferocious   digraph   laughter   stuff   different   cough   safety

stiff   forceful   tough   morphology   offer   emphasis   enough

freshest   muffin   phenomena   friction   rough   phoneme

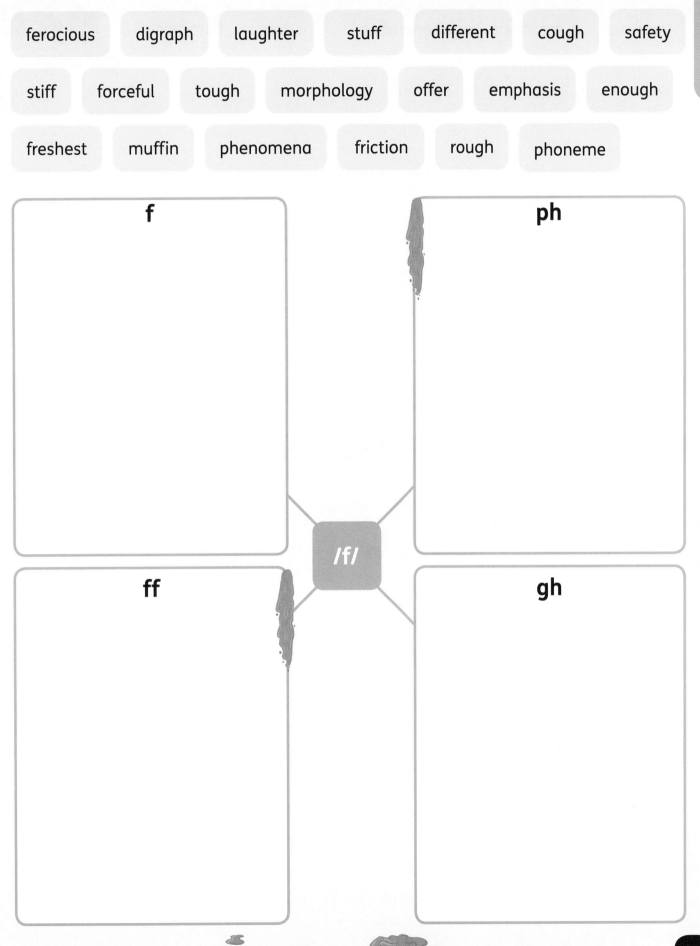

f

ph

/f/

ff

gh

2 Write these words in alphabetical order in the table. Then write a definition for each word. You may use a dictionary to help you.

ferocious   emphasis   phenomena   friction   flammable

Word	Definition

1 Use the chart to create words that start with the prefix *inter-*. Also add a suffix to each word. You may use a dictionary to help you.

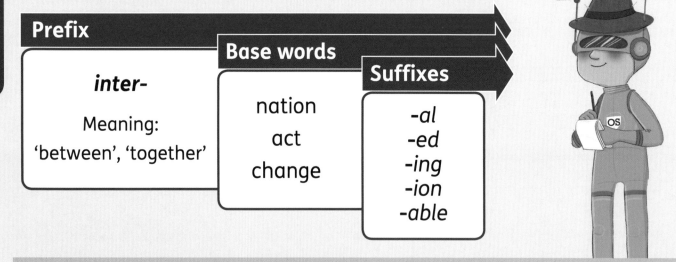

Prefix

inter-

Meaning:
'between', 'together'

Base words

nation
act
change

Suffixes

-al
-ed
-ing
-ion
-able

Words with the prefix *inter-* and a suffix

OXFORD UNIVERSITY PRESS

2 Write a definition for each word. You may use a dictionary to help you.

Word with prefix	Definition
international	
intermediate	
intersect	
interrupt	

3 Complete the sentences using the correct homophone. You may use a dictionary to help you.

flew   flu   flue

a The doctor warned it would take weeks to recover from the _____.

b Thick smoke was billowing from the chimney _____.

c We _____ to Darwin to visit our grandparents.

4 Write a sentence using each homophone.

flew	
flu	
flue	

Now try this unit's 'Bringing it together' activity, which your teacher will give you.

Phonology

1. Count the syllables in each word. Then sort the words using the table and count the phonemes.

volunteering volcano village visibility voice

violation vague verification vision venturing

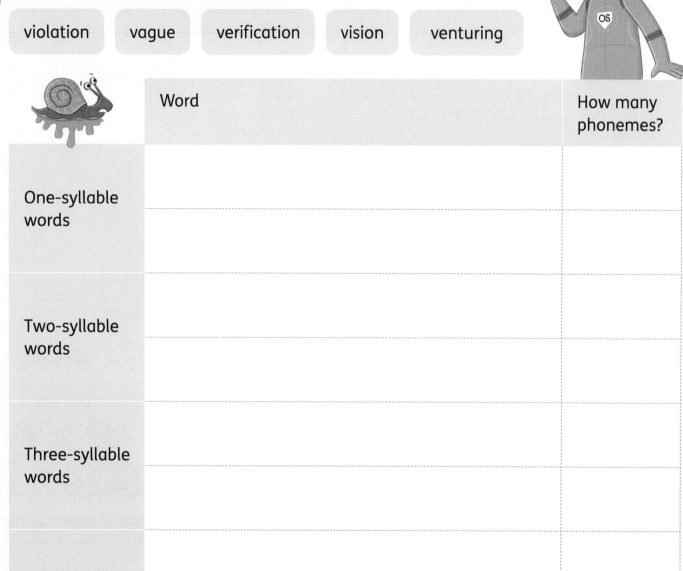

	Word	How many phonemes?
One-syllable words		
Two-syllable words		
Three-syllable words		
Four-syllable words		
Five-syllable words		

2 Write a sentence that shows alliteration using any of these words. You may add suffixes to the words if you need to.

viking	venom	vision	vague	voice	Venice	very

vacate	venture	value	visit	volcano	vibrate

vessel	vegetable	village	violate	volunteer

_____

_____

1 Write these words in alphabetical order. Then write a definition for each word. You may use a dictionary to help you.

plague	demographic	ghastly	fatigue

dinghy	analogue	league

Word	Definition

2 There are various ways to spell the **/g/** phoneme (as in the word 'get'). Find the letter patterns that spell the **/g/** phoneme in the words. Sort the words using the chart.

together   plague   demographic   biography   ghastly

catalogue   garden   gherkin   spaghetti   fatigue   gaseous

yoghurt   league   kangaroo   dinghy   analogue

/g/

gue	g	gh

Morphology

1 Complete the sentences using the correct homophone. You may use a dictionary to help you.

heard   herd

a We _____ about the opening of a new swimming pool.

b The dairy farmer milked a _____ of cows.

2 Write a sentence using each homophone.

heard	
herd	

OXFORD UNIVERSITY PRESS

3 Use the chart to create words that start with the prefix **sub-**. Also add a suffix to each word. You may use a dictionary to help you.

Prefix

sub-

Meaning:

'under' or 'beneath';
'a small part'; or
'less important'

Base words

merge

divide

conscious

Suffixes

-s
-ed
-ing
-ion
-ly

Words with the prefix sub- and a suffix

4 Write a definition for each word. You may use a dictionary to help you.

Word with prefix	Definition
submarine	
subconscious	
submerge	
subtotal	

> **Now try this unit's 'Bringing it together' activity, which your teacher will give you.**

OXFORD UNIVERSITY PRESS

GLOSSARY

accented syllable	the syllable in a word that has the strongest emphasis
	the first syllable in 'apple' and the second syllable in 'believe'
adjective	a word that tells us what something is like
	small, tall, funny
alliteration	a group of words starting with the same sound
	***b**ig **b**lack **b**ears*
base word	the smallest part of a word that is also a word on its own
	the word 'jump' in 'jumping'
blend	speech sounds that join together in a word
	/st/ *is a blend in the word 'stop'*
consonant digraph	two letters representing one consonant sound
	sh**, **ch**, **th
digraph	two letters representing one phoneme
	sh**, **ch**, **oo**, **ee**, **ie
diphthong	a kind of long vowel sound that you make by moving your mouth in two ways
	/oi/ *in 'boy',* ***/ow/*** *in 'cow'*
disyllabic word	a word with two syllables
	monster (mon-ster), sunshine (sun-shine)
etymology	the study of where words come from and how they change over time
	the word 'pizza' comes from a Latin word and an Italian dialect word meaning to clamp or stamp
graph	one letter representing one phoneme
	b**, **w**, **o
homophone	a word that sounds the same as another word but looks different and has a different meaning
	eight, ate
medial	in the middle. A medial phoneme is a speech sound in the middle of a word. This can be a medial vowel or a medial consonant.
	/o/ *is the medial phoneme in the word 'dog'*

morpheme	the smallest unit of meaning in a word
	*'jumped' has two parts with meaning (**jump** and **-ed**)*
multisyllabic word	a word that has more than one syllable
	chamber (cham-ber), trampoline (tram-po-line)
noun	a word that is a name for something, such as a person, place, animal, thing or idea
	Ali, school, cat, ball, age
onset	the sounds in a syllable before the vowel
	***b** represents the onset in the word 'big'*
prefix	letters that go at the beginning of a word to make a new word
	***un-** in 'unhappy' means 'not' (**un-** + happy = not happy)*
quadgraph	four letters representing one phoneme
	***eigh** in 'eight'*
rime	the vowel and other speech sounds at the end of a syllable
	***ig** represents the rime in the word 'big'*
schwa	an **/uh/** sound in a word
	*the **a** in 'balloon' sounds like **/uh/***
suffix	letters that go at the end of a word to make a new word
	*the **-s** in 'cats' means 'more than one cat'*
syllable	a part of a word that feels like a beat and has a vowel sound
	'weekend' has two syllables (week-end)
tense	the way a word is written that shows whether something is in the past, present or future
	'jumped' means the jumping happened in the past
trigraph	three letters representing one phoneme
	***igh** in 'might'*
unvoiced phoneme	a sound made using your breath rather than your voice
	***/th/** in 'bath'*
verb	a word for something that happens
	'play' is the verb in the sentence 'I play chess.'
voiced phoneme	a sound made using your voice
	***/th/** in 'the'*

When you have finished the activities in each unit, think about how you feel about the work you have completed.

Draw a ✓ if you feel confident using these ideas on your own.

Draw a ✗ if you feel you need to learn more.

Draw a ◯ if you are not sure.

Unit	Phonology	Orthography	Morphology
1			
2			
3			
4			
5			
6			
7			
8			
9			
10			
11			
12			
13			
14			
15			
16			
17			
18			
19			
20			
21			
22			
23			
24			
25			
26			
27			
28			

OXFORD UNIVERSITY PRESS